Go, Girls, Go!

By Anna-Sofiia Sharma

Hello! My name is Taylor, and I live in Seattle. I love ballet! My mom drives me to practice every day after school, and one day, I want to dance in New York City like the ballerinas I look up to.

Hello, I'm Jada, and I love basketball! I dribble and shoot the ball, and it's so much fun. Playing with my dad makes us even closer and makes me really happy!

Good day, I'm Julia from the Netherlands, and I love biking! Racing my brother through the streets is so exhilarating, and the wind in my hair makes me feel energized. Do you like biking too?

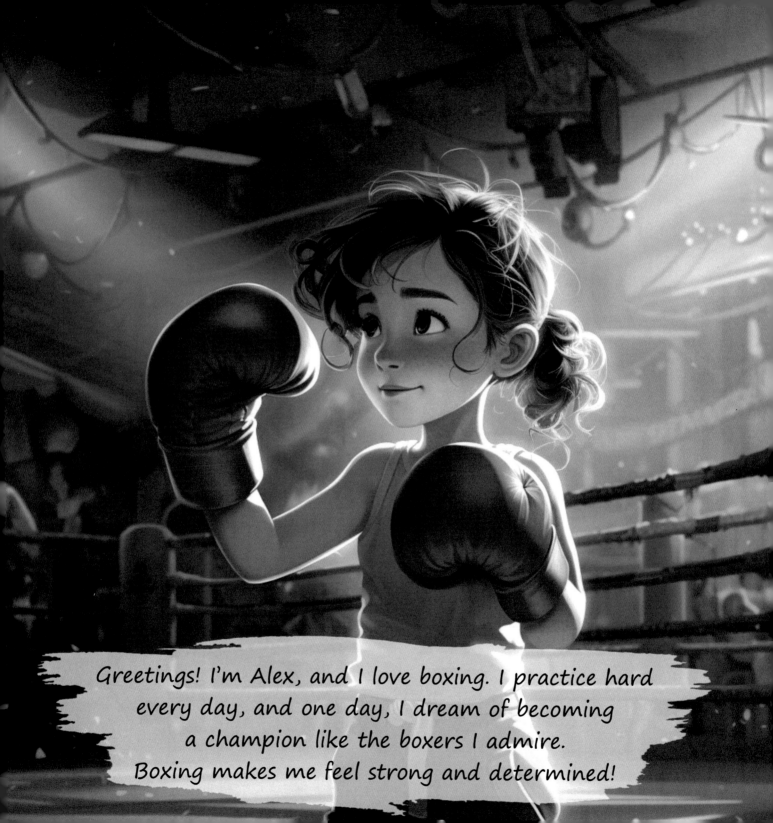

Greetings! I'm Alex, and I love boxing. I practice hard every day, and one day, I dream of becoming a champion like the boxers I admire. Boxing makes me feel strong and determined!

Hi, I'm Katie, and I love cross country running. I race with excitement, dreaming of becoming a top runner like my heroes. Cross country makes me feel free and strong!

Hola, I'm Gabriela, and I love golfing!
Swinging and putting on the green is so fun.
It makes me feel happy and excited.
I dream of becoming a golf champion one day!

I'm Li, and I love gymnastics so much!
I flip and twirl with a big smile on my face.
My dad cheers me on during practice,
and it makes me feel strong and happy!

Hey there! I'm Emma, and I love hockey! On weekends,
I practice with my brothers in the backyard.
They cheer me on, and hockey makes me
feel like a superstar!

My name is Olivia, and I absolutely love horseback riding! When I'm on a horse, I feel so free and happy. The wind in my hair and the rhythm of the horse's gallop makes me feel like I can do anything!

My name is Charlotte, and I love ice skating with my sister at the park. Gliding on the ice makes me feel like I'm flying, and it fills my heart with joy and excitement!

I'm Mia, and I really love karate! It teaches me discipline and how to stay in control. When I practice karate, I feel strong and focused, and it's like I can handle anything that comes my way!

Sophia here, and I love kayaking! It connects me with nature, and the fresh air makes me feel alive and free. Gliding on the water, I feel like I'm exploring a whole new world of adventure!

Howdy, I'm Jamie, and I really enjoy playing lacrosse! It's so much fun to run and pass the ball with my cousin at the park. Lacrosse makes me feel strong and excited, and I can't wait for our next game to score some goals together!

Hello, I'm Monica, and I love playing ping pong! It's so much fun to hit the ball back and forth with my little brother. Ping pong makes me feel happy and brings us closer together!

I'm Isabella, and I absolutely love rock climbing!
Scaling those walls makes me feel strong and adventurous.
I adore being outdoors, feeling the breeze against my face
and conquering new heights. See you on the rocks!

Hi there, I'm Margaret, and I love roller blading!
It's so much fun to glide on my wheels and explore
new areas. Roller blading allows me to see the world
in a different way, and I cherish the thrill of
discovering new places on my skates!

Salut, I'm Margaux, and I love playing rugby!
Running with the ball and being part of a team
makes me feel strong and excited.
My dream is to play for the French national team
one day and make my country proud!

Oi, I'm Bruna, and I love skateboarding through Rio!
Soaring down the hills, feeling the wind in my hair, and the
thrill of the ride makes me feel adventurous and free.
Skateboarding is my passion, and I can't get enough
of the exciting twists and turns!

I'm Ingrid, and I love skiing in my home country, Norway! The chilly air and the snowy slopes make me feel alive and happy. Going down the mountains with speed and grace fills my heart with joy and excitement!

Hey, I'm Colleen, and I absolutely love snowboarding in Oregon with my family! Coasting down the mountain with the fresh snow beneath my board fills me with exhilaration and happiness. The snowy adventures we have together are the best!

I'm Maria, and I love playing soccer with my friends! Kicking the ball and running on the field makes me feel happy and energetic. Sliding in the mud during rainy games is so much fun, and it brings us all closer together!

I'm Leilani, and I love surfing in the ocean! Riding the waves and feeling the salty breeze against my face makes me feel alive and free. Surfing is my passion, and I cherish every moment I spend catching waves!

I'm Daria, and I love playing tennis! The thrill of serving the ball and feeling the power in my shots makes me feel excited. Playing tennis with my mom is our special bonding time, and I cherish every moment on the court with her!

I'm Amara, and I love playing volleyball on the sandy beach! Feeling the warm sand on my feet and the ocean breeze in the air makes me feel happy and carefree. Spiking the volleyball brings me so much joy and excitement!

The End

Made in the USA
Middletown, DE
05 November 2023